PRIMROSE: A Celtic faery flower, symbol of early youth

Mary at the age of two

PRIMROSE TIME

A Cornish Childhood Remembered

First published 1993 by
LANDFALL PUBLICATIONS
Landfall, Penpol, Devoran, Truro, Cornwall TR3 6NW
Telephone: 0872-862581

A CIP catalogue record for this book is available from the British
Library.

ISBN 1 873443 11 0

ILLUSTRATIONS

Front cover photograph by Bob Acton: *Cornish primroses and
Cornish granite*
Inside front cover: photograph of Lelant Beach by Mary Baker
Photographs on pages 6, 9 and back cover by Bob Acton
Photograph on page 10, courtesy Mrs Eleanor Stevens
All other photographs, except where their source is
acknowledged, are from Mary Baker's family albums.
The drawings on pages 3, 11 and 43 are by Bob Acton.
All the remaining drawings, apart from those taken from
Blackie's Green Picture Book, are by Sheila Malone.

Typesetting by Bob Acton

Printed by the Troutbeck Press
and bound by R. Booth Ltd.,
Antron Hill, Mabe, Penryn, Cornwall

Mary Baker

PRIMROSE TIME

A Cornish Childhood Remembered

Landfall Publications
1993

Mary in her early eighties,
when she wrote down these memories

PRIMROSE TIME

A Cornish Childhood Remembered

If I said that my earliest memory was of setting out alone to go to the pictures, it would be a good opening to this account, but I can't say it, because I can only remember being told about it, and see in my mind my two year old self coming home to mammy, hand in hand with a tall neighbour along the sunny street.

My first true memory is of my father's dim-lit face smiling at me through the railway carriage window out of the steamy gloom of Truro station. Mother and I were travelling from Hanley to Hayle where my father had been recently appointed Excise Officer, and he came to Truro to accompany us on the last few miles of our long journey. It was near the end of November and the length of Cornwall was dark and mysterious, but father said that I would be sure to like it, and so I did.

For one thing, we stayed for some weeks with a family distantly related by marriage to my father, and there were four children, all older than me, by whom I was made very welcome and shown everything of interest which could be seen inside and outside the house. There was the harbour and the electric works and the dog next door and their beloved cat, and from the back garden

7

fence the main line trains, to which we waved with joyful vigour whether we were hidden by the steam or not. As far as I knew the trains went either this way, to Redruth, or that way, to Penzance, but the others could tell the time of day by them in a very clever way and would sing out "Din-n-n-ner" or "Tea-time", and run indoors, with me hurrying behind, to find the table laid for whichever meal they had called.

It was at this table that I ate my first pasty, and put aside a piece, carefully marked by a pattern of pastry crumbs, to be my "cold corner" at tea or supper time. All our "cold corners" were put into the sideboard cupboard, out of which came a delicious smell of pasty and saffron cake and apples and bananas and toffee. The children's father, spoken of as "Uncle" George, never seemed to sit at the table with the rest of us, but roamed restlessly about, eating very little. He was not to be restless for long, however. He had worked underground in South Africa, like many another Cornishman, and had come home with a pocket full of money, but broken in health. When he died, the money had run out, and the family knew real hardship until the children established themselves, but Christmas in their home that year was a time of delight and plenty, and happy sharing.

One thing alone I hated and feared in Hayle, and said no word of it to anyone. It was usual to be taken for walks on fine afternoons, often round the pool between Copperhouse and Phillack, and we had to make our way on the road over the lock gates. High tide filled the pool, the lock gates were closed, and opened later to allow the whole poolful to flood back to sea and deepen the Hayle river, so that boats carrying coal could come in on the tide and discharge at the power station quay. The gates had sliding trap doors in them, and fierce jets of water shot out from around the traps, even though they were closed. I felt very frightened by the pent-up power, and was always glad to get away from those gates.

Lelant pool had no gates, and the tide took its own time to flow quietly in, stay slack a while and flow out again; the village was peaceful too, so that when my parents found a "desirable villa residence" to let there, they took it and we moved into No. 1 St Neots in time for my third birthday in January 1913. Next door but one to us lived Eleanor, one month younger than me, and we very soon became close friends.

No.1 St Neots is the house on the left.

9

Eleanor in 1911, on the West Pier at St Ives

My mother has said that after the move it rained for a month without stopping and she began to doubt whether Cornwall was going to be a good place to live in after all - my father had told her of sub-tropical gardens, fuchsias growing wild, violets in winter, but nothing about the wind and rain. I stood on a chair at the front window, watching droplets at the top of the pane trickle, zig-zag and join together and race to the bottom, saying as I had been told, "Rain, rain, go away, come again another day," and when it did go away we hurried out to explore before it could come again as it so often did, not waiting for another day but soon, maybe before tea.

In the misty air the village smelled of violets, faint and sweet. Anyone who had a sheltered patch of garden planted violets in it and either sent off a box of bunches now and then to Covent Garden or sold his blooms for someone else to send with his own. And on the bank of one narrow footpath by the vicarage garden, a small gulley over-shadowed by presently leafless, dripping trees, we found our first primroses, pale and dainty.

The pathway where they grew was called Skidney and the name sounds right for what it was - narrow, steep and slippery. Those primroses were Cornwall's first offering to me and the sight and scent and feel of primroses will even now, so long after, recall the innocence of those days.

When the weather settled we took longer walks, sometimes to the ferry and sometimes to the towans, and it was there on the marram grass that I found tiny snails no bigger than silver threepenny bits. I cupped one in my hand and ran with it to mother, who admired it and said, "It's alive." I thought she said "It's a LIVE," and I decided that I must have some of these pretty little lives for myself, so I collected a lot of them and carried them home in my bucket, which I was advised to leave on the draining board until next morning, but when I went to see them my bucket was empty. They were all up the wall, some high, some low, like notes of music escaping from the black lines to make a tune, and I  loved them, but was persuaded that they probably wouldn't like to live indoors for ever, so mother plucked them off the wall and we took them back to where I had found them, and brought back a few empty shells to remind me of them.

Some things seen on the towans could not be taken home, like the little blue butterflies and the burnet moths, but on one of our walks Eleanor and I found something very beautiful and each carried one carefully in both hands, but by the time we reached the church we were very glad to put them on the wall and leave them. They were furry caterpillars, black and red and white, with funny little faces, but the hairs made our hands swollen and burning. I was rather tearful about it, but a few sweets from Mrs Bennetts' shop helped to console us, and cold water cured the pain. Mrs Bennetts said that the sweets would make it better, but that I must not eat too many "niceys" because sugar was "humoursome". I did not like to ask what "humoursome" was, and enjoyed my sweets, putting the word at the back of my mind.

Before the primroses were quite over for that year we picked a few to send to the grandmothers, some to the one in Hanley who sent me a birthday cake with silver balls and violets on it, and some to the one in Newcastle-under-Lyme who sent me a doll's pram. My father was the seventh and last child of my Hanley granny Green who came from Liverpool and liked to tell of dancing in the street when one of her brothers could be persuaded to play the flute, and she would hum the tunes to me. She sang "Oliver Cromwell is buried and dead, Hum, ha, buried and dead,"and I joined in the "Hum, ha"

part when she came to it, and could hardly wait for the end "- If you want any more you must sing it yourself, Hum, ha, sing it yourself." Grandfather Green loved music and spared a few scarce pence each week for his children to have piano lessons. With one of them playing a simple tune, granny taught the rest of them to waltz, and to dance the polka and the Lancers, in the kitchen with the mat rolled up. She knitted socks and stockings for them all, and when one of them married she knitted a bedspread in white cotton thread for a wedding gift and in due course a shawl for each baby grandchild. The family lived in Waterloo Road, the Trafalgar Road of Arnold Bennett's novels, and at intervals a tram would come grinding up from Hanley to the loop, and wait there for one to come whining down from Burslem, then both could pass and clang away. The houses had no gardens, just paved yards, but granny planted a plum stone in a drain pipe and was very pleased with the spindly little tree which grew out of it.

In the summer my Newcastle granny Schofield came to stay with us and when we couldn't go out she set about making a rag doll for me and enjoyed herself while she was working on it, especially when she sewed press-studs on its face for eyes. She dressed it like Little Red Riding Hood and although it wasn't pretty I liked it very much because I could throw it about without breaking it. Some very pretty dolls had breakable heads and were rather worrying to play with, but not Red Riding Hood: we even played "Catch" with her.

Granny wore a very dainty high collar of lace over her blouse, with pleated lace down the front, held in place by a brooch. Her blouses were close-fitting and very neat

Granny Schofield

and her black skirt, which nearly touched the ground, was full and swinging, with a pocket in the placket. She kept in that pocket a small flat tin and if I sidled up to her and held my hand out, she would open the tin and let me take out one or two of the lemon-flavoured round flat gums which she kept in it. Compared with sweets like pear drops or bull's eyes they were not particularly nice, but their name made them sound better than they really were: gelatines. As I chewed I watched her face while she talked with me. She always had time, and told me very interesting things, like always roasting a goose at Christmas because goose oil was the best thing to rub on the chest if anyone had a cold, and how she made twelve Christmas puddings, one for each month of the year, and boiled them in the copper in the back kitchen, and how she had some Bantams in her garden, pretty little hens to lay little eggs for her little girls, Sally, Laura, Mary and Mabel.

At that time I knew that she was seventy years old and that Grandfather Schofield had died when he was fifty-two, but I could not realise until I was older what his death meant to the mother of four young daughters, two of them still at school. Friends and neighbours shook their heads, I'm told, and said, "She'll never be able to stay in that house now," meaning No. 11 Mount Pleasant, opposite Newcastle High School, a boarding and day school for boys, but she did, and this is how it happened. She called on the headmaster and suggested that she should open a tuck shop in her parlour, for his pupils only, not for the general public, and he agreed. The outside of the house looked the same as ever, but the front room was stocked with sweets and chocolate, apples and pears, lemonade and ginger beer, and if a day boy wanted a hot dinner he only had to say so when he went to school in the morning and it would be ready for him at midday. Any child who was to be caned had her sympathy, and she would give him newspaper folded thickly to put in the seat of his trousers for protection. Mother told me that when any of the boarders planned a dormitory feast, Granny would pack a big basket full of very nice things and she and her older sister Sally would go quickly and quietly across to school after dark and make it fast to a rope let down by the boys, hardly daring to breathe until they were safely back indoors, because they knew that if the adventure was found out the headmaster would be very angry, and not only with the boys.

I knew nothing of all this when I looked up at her standing on the top cliff path, a black figure against the blue, her arms flung wide as she said, "Leave me! Leave me! I may never come here again, so just leave me." And we did leave her, and went home across the fields because it was quicker that way than over the links to the church, and mother had to get tea ready. When Daddy came home he said we should not have left her because she could get lost. Mother said, "She won't," and he said, "She might," but she didn't, and at last she returned, radiant, with grasses and wild flowers clipped in her arms, saying with a happy sigh, "If heaven is anything like that I shan't mind dying."

Then we all sat down for tea, one on each side of the table in the newly-decorated middle room. Father decorated it and when he was on the step ladder he sang, "When father papered the parlour," and although we liked that it was not quite right because the room wasn't a parlour and he didn't paper it. He painted the walls with something called distemper in "Pompeiian Red" and the door and window and skirting-board and picture rail and mantelpiece in white paint with a top coat of shining enamel. Mother stood around with a damp cloth and it took so long to finish the decorating that I wondered whether I should ever be allowed in that room again, but at last the paint dried and the smell blew away, and it was ready for Granny to come and have teas and dinners with us. At tea-time mother put one of her white linen cloths on the table cornerwise, and as she had made them for her bottom drawer with drawn thread work and fine knitted lace, we each had a pretty corner where the threads had crossed. We had two platefuls of bread and butter, one of brown and one of white, the thin slices cut through the middle and laid neatly on the plate one below the other. I liked the square pieces very much better than the rounded ones because they matched nicely with jam between, and I tried to move the plates so that the square slices were near to me, and even said, "No, thank you" if the round side was offered, and started on cake instead. Usually we had two kinds of cake, placed on crochet doilies, and these and the tea-tray cloth had been made by mother, all very pretty. The wedding-present teapot

with its sugar bowl and milk jug was silver, and if hot water was needed a brass kettle with a small oil lamp underneath stood on a kind of trestle which allowed it to tilt for pouring. Sometimes we had a dish of mixed sweet biscuits, and if so there would be some little A, B, Cs for me. I tried to make crumbs and keep them on the cloth, because there was a brush and crumb tray on the sideboard and I was allowed to use that when the table was cleared, but if there were no crumbs to sweep up there seemed little point in doing it.

From the lessons taken when a child my father progressed and became a very fine pianist, and soon after we were settled in Lelant he decided to buy a piano. Excise officers at that time had, as part of their duty, to

Father

deliver Old Age Pension books, and he travelled from pensioner to pensioner by bicycle, for which he was paid one penny per mile. These pennies were added to other savings and eventually he had enough to buy an upright piano, which was delivered in an enormous crate, beautifully made of oak about an inch thick. When the piano was taken out and reverently installed in the front room, the crate, on four bricks and fastened against the back wall of the garden, made a very fine house to play in with Eleanor.

Eleanor's parents were in business in St Ives and when a new baby was about to be born to them, she came to stay with her grandmother and aunt, and was so happy there that she stayed. When I hear the name Eleanor I see her little smile, silky fair hair, blue eyes, gingham pinafore and all, as if she had been the only Eleanor in the world, first and last. We collected old tins, saucepans and pots and made soup with torn up cabbage leaves, onion skins and spoonsful of rice, sago, pearl barley and such like, given to us in return for a promise never, never to drink the soup ourselves. We promised, but it seemed a pity to waste it, and the idea came to use bottles as dolls. These could be given soup and when full, made sick, and cured by medicine made of beetroot and water, and then given soup again. We soon gathered together whole families of them, dressed in oblongs of cotton print, with a hole for

the neck and tied around the middle with scraps of tape or ribbon. As all our clothes were made at home there was a good choice of oddments in mother's rag bag, and we distinguished our men and boys by dressing them in sober colours. I wanted a very small bottle to use as a baby, and asked my mother for one, but she said that she had none just now. However, I knew that there was a nice little bottle on a high shelf in the pantry under the stairs, so when mother was busy making beds we dragged a chair from the kitchen, and I climbed on to it and at full stretch, I reached the bottle. It had a label stuck on it and to my surprise was full of little white sweets. After closing the pantry door and putting the chair back, we went quietly into the dining room and divided the sweets between us, one for you and one for me, and sat on the table to enjoy them, swinging our legs, but they were disappointing. Under the thin sugary coating the middles were black and very bitter, but we made the best of it and when we came to the bitter part we spat and blew them into the empty grate. It was hit and miss, and the misses made us giggle, and the giggles brought mother, who, reading "CASCARA SAGRADA" on the little bottle, showed a controlled panic such as I had never seen before. I was not even scolded. Eleanor's grandmother calmed things down, saying, "They'ld never swallow the bitter part," and indeed the passage of time proved her to be right.

I was allowed to keep my bottle baby, provided that ON NO ACCOUNT, etc., etc., but I didn't want any more bottles, anyway. What I longed for was a real baby brother or sister. Other children had babies in the family, so why didn't I get one? Mother and I were making our way to the ferry beach one afternoon when an acquaintance beckoned us into her cottage "for a chat" as she said. I lolled about, thinking of Tom Pomeroy and his retrievers and his rowing boat and his little ferry-house smelling of tarry rope and the ribbons of seaweed streaming in the tide, when she suddenly said, "Wouldn't you like a little brother or sister to share your toys with? It must be lonely, always by yourself." I was startled that she should speak of something so painful to me and answered sharply, "No, it isn't lonely at all, because there's always me and myself." She said, "You go down the garden and look under the gooseberry bushes - you might find a baby there," and again gave mother a quick sly look which I did not like at all. I went sulking down the garden, scornful that she should tell me lies and think that I should believe her. I did not know where babies came from, but I was quite sure that they did not come from under gooseberry bushes. One thing I learned from her glances, however. Whether or not I had a baby brother or sister had something to do with my mother, but I did not like to ask her about it for fear that her reply would end " - but not for you," and after all, there were other things to think about and do in those days so full of time.

There was music. Father played the piano for an hour or two after tea on most days, Chopin, Schumann and Liszt, and we danced to it after our fashion. It could be true to say that the music danced itself into me, waking or sleeping.

There were colours. The days of the week were coloured and the months of the year, and names had colours which had nothing to do with the owners of the names, but had everything to do with the sound and the shape of the sound. For example, a Freda might have golden hair and rosy cheeks, but the word "Freda" was lilac, and "Kathleen" was pale blue, and "Elizabeth" was primrose, and so on, all different. One day we went off to Penryn by the train to spend the day with cousins of the Hayle family and among these cousins was one whose duty for that day was to look after me. She seemed very grown up to me but was probably about fourteen, and her name was Pauline. This cherry pink name was new to me and I envied my laughing chaperone bitterly, wishing that I was called by a richly coloured name instead of having to answer to Mary, all milky white. I told my mother that I wished I had been christened Pauline and she said that lots of Marys were called Polly, which was rather like Pauline, and they tried it for a day or two, but I didn't like it and refused to answer, so they stopped doing it.

Apart from not wanting to be told to put the kettle on, time and time again, there was another reason why I did not like it. A number of people in the village owned beautiful bright-coloured talking birds which had been brought from abroad by seafarers. One of these, called "Lory", spent its days nodding and bowing on its perch in Sandow's grocery shop, shouting, "Fetch a bobby! Fetch a bobby!" every time someone entered, but others that I knew of were all called "Polly", and I did not want to be called after a parrot, and be teased for talking, when I was already called a chatterbox.

I rather liked the sound of "Verily" when I heard in church "Verily, verily I say unto you -", and thought that if it was my name perhaps people would say interesting things unto me, and that whatever they said would be better than "How does your garden grow?"

It didn't grow silver bells and all that, but forget-me-nots and foxgloves and grammasows and spiders' webs and snails. I was always finding new things in it. One dazzling day I found something very new indeed, and I ran into the kitchen, calling "Mammy, come and see the pretty worm!" I was always wanting her to come and see, and she often said, "Not just now," or, "In a minute," or, "When I've finished this," but this time she came straight away to see my worm, and it was a good thing that she did so, because if she had not I should surely have carried the worm in to see her. It was beautiful, about ten inches long, black, with shiny zig-zags down its back. As soon as she saw it she said, "Don't touch it. I'll just go and ask Mr Friggins to come down and look," and she went up the garden to the back road. This was a cart track that ran behind our gardens, separating them from a field in which Mr Friggins was working, hoeing mangolds. He knew me, because I had been told that I must always say "Good morning, Mr Friggins" whenever I saw him, and he seemed to like me for that. Down he came, took a look, and said to me, "Leave it be, my lover. It's an ADDER, and if he bite you he could POISON you. Got a cat, have you?" I told him that I had got a cat, that he was black, called Toby, and I might well have said more but Mr Friggins broke in and said, "Call'n, you call'n now, and leave him see about it," so I called him and he came sailing out with his tail up like a little flag pole, ready to roll about and play, but when he saw the adder he stopped short, crept forward, padded his feet, leapt, met his teeth in its neck and gave it one wild shake. "There, see," said Mr Friggins, "he've give it a flink and broke its neck, a proper job, but it won't die till the sun go down, so I better take it away up the field."

As he took it away on mother's coal shovel I realised that there was another side to my Toby, and that the grown-ups were probably right when they said that it was he who from time to time killed a rat and laid it on the back doorstep, like a present. I have read that this behaviour is usually an activity of female cats, but was certain that he must be a "he" because he never had kittens; if he could have, I knew that he would have, because I begged him to, and he loved me. He did once give me an awful fright. When I was in bed but not already asleep the wardrobe would creak and, although mother said that it was just the wood cooling down after

a hot day, to me it sounded like someone or something trying to get out. On this particular evening I was sure that something had got out because my bed cover began to be pulled off, slowly but firmly, and I felt panic terror, stiff, like a stick and not even able to cry out. Then I heard purring and saw two little ears and two green eyes, the black parts like apple pips in the light from the Kelly lamp on the mantelpiece. He came into bed and curled up, and we both went to sleep, but he was not there in the morning. Mother knew a lot about cats and she thought that he should spend the night in his own bed in the back kitchen,and so she took him down when she was ready for bed. When we first had him she put a shoe box half full of sawdust for his convenience, and moved it a little nearer to the back door every day and when he no longer needed it during the night she put it over the grid by the outdoor water tap, where eventually it fell to

pieces, but Toby still spent his pennies where it had been. When Eleanor and I saw him go there, we ran and held him up to se the little stream he was making, and called him a teapot, but when we were told he didn't like it any more than we would, we still ran but just stood around and admired him for being so clever. We made up a "Ring o' Roses" song about him - "Toby is a teapot, Toby is a teapot," and all fell down.

Mother knew a lot about other things besides cats. Apart from cooking dinners she could make little cakes and jam tarts and potato cakes and scones for tea. She knitted socks for father and for me, and knew two different ways to "turn" the heels, and when I outgrew my socks or father's wore into holes, she roved them back from the toe, picked up the stitches and knitted new feet in them. She was a very clever dressmaker, and made for herself camisoles with lace round the neck and armholes, silk underskirts, and lovely blouses with little tucks down the front and narrow lace let in. Apart from my summer vests she made all my clothes, and I had printed cotton or gingham dresses to wear when I was playing and silk dresses or smocks for afternoons. When the weather was cool I wore sailor suits with pleated skirts, one suit made of navy blue serge and the other made of white piqué, and I also had several velvet dresses with white lace collars. Mother had to make these collars, because ready-made ones were much too big for a person of my size, and she had a lot of lace and net in keeping, bought very cheaply in the Maulage when we lived in Derby. Father's eldest sister, my aunt Fanny, lived in Leek and was able to buy remnants of velvet, and Shantung and Tussore and Jap silk from Macclesfield, and many pieces she sent for mother to make into dresses for me. These dresses all had long sleeves and when I wore the silk ones I liked to hold my arms out and run in the breeze because it made the sleeves flicker beautifully, and I did it for the pleasure.

Aunt Fanny's husband, my uncle Frank, had a shoe shop in Market Street, Leek, and every year he sent a pair of shoes for me on my birthday. I had to stand on the kitchen table, each bare foot on a sheet of notepaper, and

Mother

keep very still while mother drew a line round them to make patterns so that uncle could send shoes which would fit properly. They always did, and had to spend their first nights in Lelant on a chair by my bedside so that I could see them as soon as I woke.   One pair I was particularly proud of because they were black and very shiny, and made of PATENT LEATHER and therefore very special indeed.

Mother could do smocking, embroidery and drawn thread work, and make hairpin lace, knitted lace and crochet lace, and she knew all about materials for making clothes, with names like calico, lawn, muslin, nainsook, piqué, nun's veiling and wincey. We went to St Ives by the train when she needed to buy any materials, and after calling in to see Eleanor's mother Mrs Leddra at the shop in Fore Street, we went on to Martin's, the drapery shop. One day we went for something with a wonderful name - MADAPOLAM - to make new bolster slips. When we had our parcel we made for the wharf, down Custom House Lane and out into the wide sunlight. The tide was out, and one of the Downalong housewives had hung her washing on a line between the masts of one of the boats, pulling it high with block and tackle so that the articles could catch the breeze. There were shirts, towels, a nightdress and one or two vests, but one item of underwear interested me more than any other. It was a pair of big white bloomers which looked as if the dressmaker had tired of sewing them before joining the two legs together, and had just set them into a band, with ends like an apron string to tie around the waist, and the little puffs of wind made them kick about and dance very boldly. I decided that when I grew up I would never wear anything like that.

Although I was not aware of it at that time, I now realise that we small children were looking, listening, thinking and deciding, every minute of our waking days, no matter what else we were doing or how engrossed we might seem to be in doing it. Of course, we were being told a lot of things, all the time, but some of what we were told was not true. I don't mean being told that babies were to be found under gooseberry bushes or that eating crusts would make hair curl, because I think that we were not supposed to believe these things, but to stop asking awkward questions and eat up our crusts. No, I am thinking particularly of the matter of the paddling drawers. One of our visitors came back from St Ives with something in a paper bag and even before I could begin to ask questions she said, "There! It's for you," so I opened the bag and took out rompers of a sort, made in the same material as my sponge bag and smelling of mackintosh. They had elastic round the legs and waist, and a bib which tied with tapes to the waist at the back. I was told that they would keep my clothes dry when I was paddling, and I was very pleased, and tried them on. We frequently joined our friends in Hayle for a day on their beach and crossed the ferry to get there. If we were going to their house first we went to the Weir and walked, over dreaded lock gates to Foundry Square and up by the station to Harbour View, but this day we crossed right over the river and walked round to meet them all at the beach proper. There was Gertrude, Kathleen, Tommy, Una and their new little sister Rachel, and with their mother, my mother, our two visitors and me, we were a lively crowd. As soon as I had been tucked into the paddling drawers and the tapes were tied, I ran for the sea, jumping over the little waves and prancing this way and that to make showers of spray in the sunlight. I was having a lovely time and when I noticed mother at the edge of the water and I ran to tell her about it, she said, "Just look at your clothes! They'll all have to come off." And they did come off, every single thing, even my vest, and were laid out to dry in the sun, while I sat hunched in my summer coat, very ashamed, and very resentful. I felt deceived.

However, when we children sat astride the arms of the settee and said that we were riding horses, or crawled under the table and said that we were in a cave, we were not telling lies. It was just pretending, a different matter altogether, and most grown-ups had given up doing it, which seemed a pity, but my father was good at it, and at making up stories and rhymes as well. When on a Sunday morning I climbed into my parents' bed and slid down between them, he said that if we all faced one way we could be like spoons in the kitchen table drawer: I could be a tea spoon, mother could be a dessert spoon and he would be a serving spoon. Then he told all about John Oliver, like

"John Oliver's nose was long,
John Oliver's nose was long,
John Oliver's nose reached down to his toes,
John Oliver's nose was long."

When he had described John Oliver's hair "- there wasn't much there -" and his nails "- the colour of snails -" and his eyes "- like big butterflies -" it was time for dessert spoon to get up and dress, and go downstairs to make breakfast. In spite of John Oliver's seeming to be rather ill-favoured, I liked him, and suggested other features for father to make rhymes of, but "ankles" and "elbows" and "fingers" and "thumbs" didn't fit in very well, so father said, "Let's do some limericks instead. Think of a place." I didn't then know many places, so father decided on Hayle, and made this:

"There was a young fellow from Hayle,
Who went for a cruise on a whale.
By night and by day
He went his own way,
And steered it with strings on its tail."

I could see that whale with the young fellow sitting on its head, sailing past the ferry and us all waving and the young fellow waving back, but before they sailed "down

around" to St Ives or "up around" to Godrevy, a voice called, "Time for tea spoon to wash and dress," and I had to get up, and be helped to get ready for breakfast.

This began with a small bowl of porridge, or something new and healthy called "Grape Nuts", which came in an orange-coloured packet with a lot of printing on it, and no pictures. Porridge was made from "Quaker Oats" and there was a picture on the packet of a man in a three-cornered hat. Sometimes father would sing to the tune of "The Ash Grove",

"There once was a Quaker
Who lived in Long Acre,

33

And he was a maker
Of car-ri-age wheels,"

and I thought that he was referring to the Quaker Oats
man in some way or other, but when I read Pepys' diary I
found out that Long Acre was the place where carriage
wheels were made, so maybe he made it up for fun, and
used the word "Quaker" to rhyme with "Long Acre". Who
knows? Anyway, on Sundays we often had a boiled egg
each, and brown and white bread and butter, and apostle
spoons to eat the eggs with, and father would tap his egg
around the top in a rhythm, and say, "What is this tune?"
And I would guess, and I was always right. Anyone
might think that it was very clever of me to be always
right, but it wasn't, because the tune was always "Good
King Wenceslas".

On weekdays father had no time to play games and sing
songs. His office was in Hayle at the Custom House, a
small building by the lock gates opposite St Elwyn's
church, and when he was working there he went down to
the ferry and was rowed across by Tom Pomeroy, but if
the tide was out Tom would carry him on his back to the
weir. If it was a day for dealing with Old Age Pension
Books he would cycle up and away, and make a wide loop
through St Ives and Towednack, and then come sailing
down from Cripplesease, and the only uphill part then
was from Trevethoe Gates through the village to St Neots
Villa, our house. He wore lightweight boots and puttees,
and every morning I went down on hands and knees to
watch the winding round and round of these puttees,
every turn precise and slow. It seemed to me an
important workday ritual, and the very name "puttees"
had a sound of dignified sobriety. When the sun shone he

wore a straw hat, fastened to the lapel of his jacket by a clip on a very fine black cord, and he looked very jaunty as he waved "Goodbye". He came home for dinner at midday and we had a hot meal of shepherd's pie or fishcakes or rissoles or liver and bacon, with vegetables, followed by milk pudding or fruit and custard, or pancakes with brown sugar and lemon juice. People in the village did not care for liver, and Mr Olds the butcher gave it away to anyone who would take it, and it became a favourite meal of mine, and mother liked it especially because of the saving in her housekeeping money.

Father always had tales to tell about his morning's work, who he had met and what they had said, and sometimes these tales interested me, as when someone said, "Wish'd weather," or "It'll make rain when the tide turns," or "I was some frightened," meaning "surprised". When in St Ives father could not at first deliver pension books quickly because the name of the recipient was not always what he was called, - "Mr Whatsisname" was "Mr Whatsicall", and father had to learn all the nicknames of the "Whatsicalls" before he could give them their books.

When I lost interest in the conversation I amused myself by looking at my funny face reflected in my pudding spoon. It was possible to make the ferry out of plums and custard, and sweep the pink tide in between the shores, and put the plums for cliffs, and gaze at it until told, "Eat up your pudding," and I came back, and ate the plums, to discover once again that I would marry a soldier sometime, and wear muslin, but I did not believe it really, so I only laughed when the plumstones said that I should go to my wedding in a wheelbarrow!

It was very easy to learn simple things by heart, and although it was not all simple I learned the Lord's prayer and said it every evening before I got into bed. The part which I found most puzzling was the trespasses, and it became a little clearer in a funny way. An aunt of the Hayle children came over to have tea with us, and mother decided that as the weather was so lovely the three of us would walk to Trevethoe Farm for some cream to have with bread and jam as a treat. So off we went, down to the bottom of the village, through Trevethoe Gates and up the winding drive between the Forty Acre Field on the left and the cricket ground on the right. When we came almost level with the house, on the left a large shrubbery was separated from the field on one side and the driveway on our side by an iron railing, and a post with a notice board on it stood alongside. I asked what it said on the board and was told "Trespassers Will Be Prosecuted", which meant that the squire did not mind us walking along the drive but we must not TRESPASS into his shrubbery. That seemed to explain the difficult bit in the Lord's prayer and I decided that I would not do any trespassing and so not have to be forgiven. Then, seemingly from nowhere, an enormous swan, with his toes turned in and his neck stretched out, came towards us, looking very angry, and when he began to hiss and arch his great wings mother said to me, "Get through the railings," which I did very quickly, while she climbed up and sat on the top bar, but our visitor screamed and had to take hold of the bar and hop up with her feet together because she was wearing a hobble skirt, and could not bend her knees to climb up. After a while the swan decided that we were harmless and wandered away, our friend hopped down, and we went on to the farm for our cream, and I thought that if to trespass was

no worse than what I had done, why did it seem so serious in one's prayers? I decided to say my prayers as if I could understand it, because some people said that prayer every Sunday without looking puzzled and I felt that I would perhaps grow into it in time, so I pushed it into the side of my mind, like putting a hard sweet into my cheek, and got on with other things, new every day.

After primroses came cowslips, smelling like apricots, and lilies of the valley, sweet peas, pinks, mignonette and wallflowers. Then there were all the different leaves to pinch for their scents: the mints, parsley, sage, old man and geraniums. On the way to Tren Crom, at Splattenridden, there was honeysuckle, and wild roses, and sometimes the smell of foxes, and the first drops of rain made little beads in the dust. I was enchanted with it all, and so that I could stay with it I decided not to grow up, but time and school overcame me and I had to learn many things that I really did not want to know, and read things that I really did not want to read, but when I came upon, "I know a bank whereon the wild thyme blows" I felt wonderful, because I knew such a bank, on the links behind the church, and could remember lying there to breathe the scent, and seeing among the thyme forget-me-nots with flowers no bigger than pin-heads, and a snail eating tiny mouthfuls of a daisy leaf.

In the other St Neots Villa lived Miss Permewan and her maid Janey, who seemed to like me, and when I went out of the back gate I could go into their garden, down the path and into their kitchen, which was more interesting than ours because it had a knife cleaning machine in it, and when the knives were safely installed Janey would let me turn the handle, and gave me a sweet for helping her. One sunny day I decided to go and see her, and noticed that there were some lovely red flowers growing up bamboos. I picked a nice bunch and took them back for mammy. She was not as pleased with them as I had hoped, and took me round to tell Miss Permewan that I was sorry for picking her beans. She was very kind and smiling, and said that it didn't matter at all, so I promised not to do it again, and she said that I might visit Janey any time I liked. It was a pity about the beans.

When the gleaming blackberries had come and gone, it was time for violets to begin to bloom again, and then, soon after, came Christmas, and I hung up my stocking. It was really one of Daddy's socks, because my own were too small to hold anything, and in it was an apple and an orange, some sweets and some nuts wrapped in silver paper, but on my bed was a doll's tea-set, a wax doll, a small round box with a handle at one end and a flat box which had "Harbutt's Plasticene" printed on it, as I was told. In it were several sticks of a brick-red pliable material, and Eleanor and I broke bits off and rolled them into balls, and that was all until father came to look and said, "I'll make something for you," and we watched. He took a whole stick and rolled it and rolled it and rolled it between his palms until he had a long sausage tapered at both ends.

He then laid one end down like a tail and stuck two small feet on to it, reared the body up and supported it on two legs and used the rest of it to make an arched neck and a small head in which he made two little holes for eyes. "There," he said. Naturally enough we asked what it was, and he said, "It's a DIPLODOCUS, a DINOSAUR, and I'll tell you about them another day," so we had to wait until another day came, but they were very easy to make, and having seen how to do it, we made some and put them to walk along the window sill.

I asked what the round box with the handle was for, and was told that it was a musical box. It made a noise like "Tink, tank," slowly or quickly according to how the handle was turned, but compared with the sparkling notes which father made his piano say, I did not think that "Tink, tank" was musical, so we pulled it to pieces and hid it away.

For my birthday in January I had a cake, this time with golden balls round the edge in a zig-zag, and Cinderella's coach in the middle, and new shoes, some coloured chalks and a real book, with hard covers, called Blackie's Green Picture Book. The pictures were by Hassall, and so "right" that I could easily imagine myself being with the characters he depicted. I never tired of it and happily "improved" his work with my chalks.

Primroses came to join the last of the violets, and soon it was Pancake Day, and father tossed his very high. Mother was more fearful and turned them over with a fish slice. Then it was Easter, and mother made for me a "coat frock" using a length of white Jap silk which my aunt Fanny had sent. The bodice of this coat frock was lined to the waist, long-sleeved, with a skirt pleated all round, and bodice and skirt set into an embroidered waist band, and the front fastening neatly concealed. This garment was made especially to be worn at church on Easter Sunday morning. I had a straw hat trimmed with daisies to wear with it, and watched with interest while pale blue ribbon was threaded through the broderie anglaise on my Sunday knickers and petticoat. Eleanor was just as fine too, in her Leghorn hat with streamers, and we sat and fidgeted together. Some families in the village always had their first picnic on Good Friday afternoon, and when all the food was eaten, filled the baskets with primroses and wild violets neatly bunched and tied with cotton, to make the church a bower for Sunday. The wide window ledges were cushioned with them, and the church nestled so low that through one window on the north side I could see tall grasses waving.

BLACKIE'S GREEN PICTURE BOOK

When the organ began to play and everyone stood up, Eleanor and I stood up too, and knelt down for "Let Us Pray," but when the vicar in his surplice climbed into the pulpit and began to speak, half of me tried to sit still and understand what he was saying while the other half was away to the tall grasses, running, flying, through the kissing gate, across the links, over the footbridge to the towans, the rabbit holes, and headlong down the cool sliding sand to the beach. But I did not reach the sea because people began to turn pages of their hymn books and stand up, and I and myself were together again, trying to make the sound of the last hymn more interesting by putting my fingers in and out of my ears in quick time. At last, at joyful last it's over, everybody going home. Eleanor and I pushed and sidled our way out, under green bushes to the lane, where we waited. "Hold hands, and don't run," we were told, so we held hands and didn't run, but skipped instead. Under arching trees, an open gateway led to pasture for cows and stabling for horses. "Mind you don't step in something," called someone, but we did not need to be warned about the "something" which was always there, and we skipped on, singing gleefully. People behind us were smiling and nodding and saying agreeable things about us, but we were not singing "Little Bo Peep" or "Humpty Dumpty", but an original lyric which went "Hoss mess, hoss mess, hoss piddle, hoss piddle," and this was the cause of our delight. We were not dear little girls, but rude little girls, in spite of our frills, and ribbons threaded through. And when we heard the word "hospice" for the first time we could hardly believe it, and whispered it with a hand over the lips, and twirled about in rapture.

That Easter was our second in Lelant, and the summer

was a very busy one for my mother as so many relations from Staffordshire came to spend a holiday with us.

These relations usually came in twos, an aunt and an uncle, and they all knew me from times that I could not remember. They seemed to think that I should be as amused as they were themselves by remarks made by me a long, long time ago, when I was only two, and not four, but I wasn't amused at all, and just felt silly. One story they told to each other over and over again went like this: "Do you remember when we were going for a drive in Joe Hind's new motor-car and we were held up by a herd of cattle in a lane, she asked why cows don't wear knickers?" And someone else was sure to say, "Oh yes, and Laura says that the first time they took her to church she asked, in a loud voice, why the singing boys were wearing nighties!" They laughed and looked at me with their heads on one side. I felt that should not be made fun of because of what I had said when I was too young to know any better.

The little boy who lived next door to me was two years of age, and he didn't seem able to say anything except "Coffee Pot." This was an enamel coffee pot given to Eleanor and me to play with, and he liked it, and wanted it, and every fine morning there he was again at the back gate, calling "Coffee Pot, Coffee Pot!" We always told him to go away but one day it seemed that he meant to stay there for ever and ever, so I took the pot and Eleanor took a little old saucepan, and having filled both with water from the tap in the yard we climbed up the gate and emptied them over him. When his angry mother came round to tell my mother what we had done "- soaked to the skin -" Eleanor and I were in disgrace, and told to let him have the coffee pot to play with, but when he had it he only walked around the garden with it, flapping the lid.

I had to admit to myself that when I was three, one whole year older than my little neighbour, I was still riding in a push-chair for part of the way if the family was going to Tren Crom for a picnic, but now that I was four I walked all the way, there and back again. When it was time to make for home we usually came down the hill to Bowl Rock, and I hurried to the cottages there, because in front of them was a small table with a white cloth on it, and a cloam jug of home-made lemonade, and glasses. Someone of our party always bought a glassful for me and I sat on the wall to drink it. About thirty years ago I sat on that same wall and an old lady came across the yard and said, "Tired, are you?" I explained to her that I was just recalling the time long ago when I had sat there drinking lemonade, and she said, "It would have been me that gave you that. Mother made it and I sold it, for a bit of pocket money. We never had much in those days, nor ever went anywhere much either, only down Splattenridden to St Erth of a Saturday night, sparking with the boys, but they were good times, better than now. People race up and down here in their motor-cars as if they don't know where they're going." I agreed and we waved each other "Goodbye", but when I was the little girl on the way home from a picnic I knew exactly where I was going: up the narrow lane, past the pump, to Beersheba Farm and across the field, over the stile and into the lane at Mount Douglas. This lane was very special and well worth the climb up from Trevarrack because there was MONEY to be found there. The grown-ups strolled along, saying "Lovely weather," or "Look at that sky," and then suddenly one of them would stop and point to the ground, and I would run and find a real halfpenny, and another and another, maybe six or seven, until we reached the main road at Longstone. There were no more to find

45

Auntie Mary Schofield

after that, so I did not mind if Daddy gave me a piggy-back and I don't think he minded much either because it was downhill all the way home, or nearly.

When we went to Tren Crom we usually made for a specially good place, sheltered by rocks, facing west and fairly level, and we came to think of it as "our" place, but one day we found that someone had been there before us. Apples and oranges had been thrown about, sausage rolls crumbled up, chocolates stamped on and cigarettes torn into pieces. Mother said "Oh" (the kind of "Oh" that means "I see"), "a lovers' quarrel." Father said "Haha," and taking some of the tobacco from the torn cigarettes, put it into his pipe and lit up. I thought it smelled funny and asked why, and he said, "They're Abdullas, Turkish. Very expensive." I couldn't help feeling that those lovers must be very silly people not to have had their picnic first and their quarrel afterwards, as they had brought such nice things to eat, and expensive cigarettes as well.

Mother's younger sister, my Auntie Mary, came to live with us and taught at St Erth village school. It was very pleasant for me to have another playmate, even if she was a grown-up, and to have a schoolteacher auntie put me on a level with Eleanor, whose Auntie Nellie Williams was a teacher at Lelant village school, so we each had a teacher living with us. My Auntie Mary played the piano and chose popular songs of the time and encouraged me to sing them with her, which I did with pleasure and enthusiasm, but many of the songs seemed odd, even silly. "They call me Ginger, gin, gin, gin, gin, Ginger," for instance - why ever should all the girls love a hot old, red-headed man? And -

"Come, birdie, come and live with me,
You shall be happy, gay and free.
You shall be all the world to me,
If you will come and live with me."

I loved all the birds, every single one, and they were all happy, gay and free already. I would have gladly gone to live with them, swooping about in the sunshine, lighting on the clothes line for a swing before shooting up on to the roof, but to think of one of them going to live in a house - no, no, never. Then there was this one -

"Hello, hello, who's your lady friend,
Who's the little girlie by your side?
I've seen you with a girl or two,
Oh, oh, oh I am surprised at you!"

And this -

"Who were you with last night
Out in the pale moonlight?
It wasn't your sister, it wasn't your ma,
Ah, ha, ha, ha haha, haha!"

These songs were fun to sing, but I could not understand the pictures that came into my mind when I sang the words, so I pushed them aside with other inexplicable grown-up things, like smoking tobacco and wearing hair-nets and corsets, all to be considered at some later time.

Perhaps because I loved birds so much, father decided that we should have a pair of doves and he ordered a dovecote to be made by the village carpenter but the doves were delivered before the dovecote was finished and had to live for the time being in a wooden box with wire netting on one side of it. This was hung on the scullery wall above the sink and very sad the pretty pair looked, perched in it. One evening father said that they ought to

Miss Nellie Williams and Eleanor

come out of the box for a little while to stretch their wings, but not to fly out of doors until the dovecote was in place for their homecomings. Doors and windows of kitchen and scullery were closed and father carefully took the birds and perched one on mother's shoulder and the other on my aunt's stiffly pointing forefinger. We all smiled at each other and at the pretty creatures, bright-eyed and trustful, but one thing had been forgotten. It was late September and there were many flies "coming indoors out of the cold" as people said. Every house had a flypaper in the kitchen, and there was one in ours, hanging from the ceiling. Some slight sound or movement alarmed mother's bird, which took off and, after a few frightened flaps, stuck to the flypaper. The other bird did likewise and the weight of them both caused the flypaper to fall to the floor where they bound themselves up in it. Suddenly I was under everyone's feet, in the way, helpless and very frightened, and it was good to escape to bed, trusting that it really would be "better in the morning". I don't think that it was very much better for the doves, however. They perched side by side in their box, two pairs of sad eyes only just able to look out over the puff-balls of down sticking to their beaks. Mother hooked the box outside on the wall of the house for their daily change of air and while we were having dinner they forced a way out and fled away, and we never saw them again. Next day the dovecote was delivered, and Eleanor and I played with it as a kind of doll's house but not for the bottle dolls - they were all too tall for the doorways.

From time to time I looked up into the faraway blue, wondering where those birds would have flown: the sky seemed to go on for ever. The hymn said that there was a Friend for little children above the bright blue sky, and I knew who that was. It was Jesus, who sitteth on the right hand of God, but I was puzzled, because the Holy Ghost could probably float about, but where could the Father and the Son live? They could not live on clouds because clouds were not always there, and when they were there they changed all the time, from faces to animals, to mountains, to sailing boats, to icing on a cake, sometimes streaming like silky white or grey hair in the wind, and always like the shapes of music in the mind. It was beautiful and mysterious, and it all belonged to me, and I was sure that one day I would find out more about God and Jesus. They had to be somewhere, and maybe the doves had gone to them. I hoped so.

The weather was glorious all summer long, until August came with milky skies and colours of Jersey cows and corn and dust. Eleanor's uncle came home on leave from the navy and he took us to have splits and jam and cream at Granny Ashton's tea garden at Hawke's Point, in one of the little summer houses above the Nut Grove. We went to the church, through the kissing gate, across the golf links to the footbridge over the railway, just as I had done in imagination when sitting through the sermon on Easter morning, but now we turned to the left and made our way across the towans, keeping close to the railway line but outside the wire. Uncle Guy strode along, but we ran ahead, lagged behind, bumped into each other, pranced about like puppies and even fell over on purpose in joyful foolery. The smell of sunshine, marram grass and sand was everywhere. At last the towans ended and the cliff began, its edge hidden by hazel trees dwarfed and rounded by onshore winds, shutting out the sunshine from the path, steep, narrow and rough. We walked delicately into the miniature forest as into a fairy story, and scarcely spoke, for the need of listening and watching. I was not sure what I was listening and watching for, but I ducked my head and ventured forward warily, no longer bounding like a puppy but picking my way like a kitten in a new surrounding. It was a place for whispering, enchanted, a child-size forest, and at the far end, where we came out and crossed the railway line, there were doll-sized strawberries to be picked and eaten with relish when the time was ripe. Once over the line we were soon in the tea garden, being greeted by smiling Granny Ashton and shown into one of the summer houses. Eleanor and I made haste to climb on to the window seat and gaze between the strands of honeysuckle at our white beach, the deep blue River Hayle, Gwithian towans and Godrevy, and only the arrival of a wide trayful of cream teas took our attention from the blue and the brilliance. After tea we walked steeply up, and over to the railway station where it said CARBIS BAY in letters made of rosettes of flowers growing in gravel. The train puffed its way gently round from St Ives and when we were on board round it went in the cutting, past the little tea-houses, and there was our beach again, the shallow sea spread out like a silk petticoat ruffled with white water. Soon we were fussing across the towans.

Lelant Beach - an old picture postcard

Over the small bridge where Tom Pomeroy the ferryman waved to us, and sliding to a halt at Lelant. As we jumped down I spelled it out - "L-E-L-A-N-T", and toiled slowly up station hill in the cool shade, hearing the "squa-a-wk" of the rooks high up in the trees. I felt that it was all mine, and I was proud and happy, and tired.

Uncle Guy took my auntie Mary out sometimes, for whole days, and we felt a little jealousy then, because we were not invited, but when they brought us each a neat little serpentine brooch from the Lizard, we felt happy again because the brooches were set in REAL SILVER, and had to be kept very carefully, so we were told.

We played a lot of games with verses to say, like, "My mother says - " and "Johnny caught a fish alive," and we were told to say some rather prim things, like "Little birds in their nests agree, and so must we." When I heard how mother and father birds made nests to lay eggs in, and lined them with bits of wool and feathers to make a comfortable bed for their nestlings, I decided to do something very kind for them. I took a card of mending wool from mother's work basket, cut it all up into little pieces, and hid it. Then I felt the corners of pillows and cushions in the house and pulled out all the feathers I could find, and put them with the bits of wool in a paper bag. Then I sauntered into the garden, scattered my gifts in a far corner and sat down to watch, but as it was September the birds were not interested. I was very disappointed, but had to keep quiet about it, because of the wool, and when mother looked in her work basket for wool to mend some socks, and said, "That's funny. I was sure I had a card of grey," I became very quiet indeed, but she just went down to Mrs Bennetts' to buy some more and didn't ask me if I knew where it could be. I only told lies if I absolutely had to, so I was very glad that she didn't ask and I didn't have to tell any.

Auntie Mary sometimes sang songs which were meant for children, like this one:

"Hush, here comes the sand man,
Quick, it's MR SAND MAN.
Now, you children, run up the stairs
Put on your nighties and say your prayers
And ride with Mr Sand Man
Till daylight comes again
And see all the wonders of Wonderland
From the Dreamland Train!"

I was polite about it, but didn't like it much, or feel at home with it. "Wee Willie Winkie" was more to my taste.

Wee Willie Winkie as portrayed by Blackie's Green Picture Book, with additional decoration by me.

When Christmas drew near Auntie sang:
"Hang up the baby's stocking,
Be sure you don't forget,
The dear little dimpled darling
Has ne'er seen Christmas yet!"
I thought that to sing a song like that to me was unkind
- surely everyone knew that I longed for a dimpled
darling, and it couldn't possibly be a reminder for anyone
to hang a stocking for me, because I was going to be five
in January!

Mary and Eleanor reunited after nearly eighty years

This meant that I would then be ready to start school, but
it was going to be different for me: I should stay at home
all the time and have lessons with Auntie. Mother had
sung the alphabet with me in two different versions, so I
knew that, and from repeatedly asking, "What does that

say?" I had begun to read. As well as toys and things to eat I had in my stocking a pencil box with an india-rubber and a ruler, and for my birthday I had my lovely iced cake, new shoes and a doll, but also an exercise book with double lines so that I could do my "pot-hooks", and another one with squares for "sums". The doll was very beautiful, with a china head, curly hair, and eyes which opened and closed. I called it my BIG DOLL, and mother made clothes for it, miniatures of the clothes she made for me.

In my two previous Cornish years I had been too young to notice that if the wind blew at the time of my birthday it usually blew very hard indeed, but this year I did notice it. The beach was two fields, the golf links and the towans away, but the raving gale drove sand through the window sashes, and under the front door and the vestibule door, and when mother put a rolled-up blanket to keep the sandy draught back, the wind blew it away as if laughing at her. The hedges and trees had turned their backs to it long since, and stayed that way, ready. Some of these curling hedges were blackthorn, and when in March they covered themselves in white blossom it was

called the blackthorn winter, but I thought that they were like waves of the sea, caught in the act of breaking. When the strong winds blew we didn't go to the beach, and although I was told that the sea could be rough, it was many years before I saw it so, and felt the cliff shudder from the weight of it. I only knew it as friendly, the small waves chasing each other until time to slide back, leaving things for us to find at the tide line. Once, but once only, it brought hundreds of small jellyfish, like glassy marbles, and we were told not to touch, but we didn't want to anyway, because they looked slippery. Always there was something interesting, and I can see myself bent like a hairpin for most of an afternoon, finding and collecting. Mussel shells in pairs looked like giant bluebottles, and other paired shells looked like butterflies, especially the dainty

little pink ones, which we prized above all the others. Then there was cuttlefish bone, and the cases of dog-fishes' eggs, and seaweed like cows' tails, and some like green ribbon, and small heaps of bladderwrack where

the ghostly sand-hoppers lived. We did find bottles occasionally, but never one with a message in it. There was always something to take home for a treasure, and even father would carry pieces of driftwood to burn in the sitting-room fire grate, for the rich blue glow which came from the salt in it. Sometimes we had our picnic just round The Point from the ferry beach, and some other times we went across the links, down to the beach at the end of the towans and settled ourselves on the stones below Granny's Bonnet, a small shelter which stood at the Nut Grove. From here to Hawke's Point the beach was different, but no less interesting. Instead of towans there was cliff, with water trickling down from the Wishing Well, and a gentle slope of stones at the bottom, before the sand began. One or two rocks peaked out of this sand, and the tide left pools around them, usually warmer than the sea itself, perfect for paddling and dabbling in, but for me, the very best place was Hawke's Point itself. It was mysterious. Water ran out of an enormous cleft in the cliff, its rocky bed stained orange-gold, and half-way back but half-way up, was another cleft like a huge keyhole, and the lip of that one was stained jade green. I was told that those clefts were ADITS from mines, where miners dug tin and copper. The sun left that part of the beach first, and in the cool shadow it became for me somewhere outlandish, but wonderful. Once when the slow tide came round from Carbis Bay and reached my knee height, I saw that it had brought a shoal of very tiny fish, like darning needles. Keeping the same distance from each other and moving in a straight line, they swam quickly, then all stopped, as if listening, and swam, and stopped again, until they saw my legs, and then all turned, and swam, and stopped, and swam away, into a secret world, and I marvelled at them for never bumping into each other.

Although we belonged to the church, my mother began to go down to the chapel hall one afternoon a week, carrying a basket of rock cakes when it was her turn to do so, and I stayed at Eleanor's house until she came home, with several flannelette night shirts in a paper bag under her arm, cut out and ready to be machined together. I asked many questions and was told that the shirts were for wounded soldiers to wear in hospital, that the Germans wounded them because there was a war and fighting with guns, and that Red Cross nurses looked after them and made them better. I wanted to be a Red Cross nurse, so an apron and cap were made out of an old pillow case, and crosses of red material tacked on. Wearing these, I stood in the doorway of St Neots to let everyone see me, and while I was there a small platoon of soldiers came clattering down the road, singing and waving and blowing kisses, and I looked down and waved back. Twenty-five years later I looked down on more soldiers, singing, whistling and waving to me in the autumn sunshine as they marched cheerfully down Weeke Hill to Dartmouth. I waved, but my eyes stung with tears at the pity of it, all over again. Married life had been hard for us, and when my third baby was born I was always very busy, so I often went to bed when I could feel that all the day's work was done, and I might amuse myself with a book or the wireless. I liked to tune in to Warsaw, as there was a recital of Chopin's music in the late evening and it reminded me of blissful evenings in bed at home, but one night as I turned the knob I was stayed by an urgent voice which said, "This is the voice of Republican Spain. Listen, take warning and help us. If we are overcome, the whole of Europe will be plunged into war." I felt very afraid and helpless, and now it was as the voice had said, and Europe was at war. But "war" meant nothing to be afraid of when I proudly stood on the top step in my Red Cross nurse's uniform, and I well knew what it was to be a wounded soldier - you grazed your knee and shed a few tears, and sucked a sweet while the sore place was bathed and bandaged with Homocea or Germolene ointment and you were told "Now you are a wounded soldier," and given a kiss before you ran off to show your stiff leg to anyone interested enough to look. In following the devices and desires the pain was soon gone, but someone's brother came home very lame because he lost his toes with frostbite, and he stayed wounded and could not be a soldier any more, and someone else was "missing believed killed." These items of overheard news were too disturbing to dwell on, but were like the first drops of rain at a picnic.

I made fair progress with reading, and for Christmas I was given, among other things, a copy of "Alice's Adventures in Wonderland", and liked it so much that I was given "Through the Looking-glass" for my birthday. I was still young enough to believe, or at least hope, that magic was possible, and I climbed up to the mantelpiece, and although I couldn't get through the mirror I felt it was worth trying, just in case. Young children have to get used to being told, quite often, that what they are saying is wrong, or silly, or funny, but in the Alice books it is the creatures, animals and people, who say wrong and silly and funny things, and on hearing this the child can, for once, feel very clever. I did not think that Alice always had a pleasant time in these stories, but I had already unwillingly accepted the fact that in real life things were not always happy, and when I knew the stories well, I could smile, because it was all right in the end, when she woke up. I was sure that when Lewis Carroll wrote "The Walrus and the Carpenter" he had seen them in his mind's eye eating their oysters on our beach, and I saw them there in my mind's eye, too, every time we we went down, and when he made the Mock Turtle sing, "There is another shore, you know, upon the other side," I felt that he must have been there, because there it was, the other shore, and it was called Gwithian. These two books were read to me so often that I learned all the songs and verses without even trying, and enjoyed repeating them to myself, just for fun. For two reasons, I especially liked JABBERWOCKY.

" 'Twas brillig, and the slithy toves
Did gyre and gimble in the wabe,"

and so on and so on. Firstly, the words of these verses slung themselves together like rare fancy beads on a necklace, and secondly, and secretly, I knew where the slithy toves could be found. It was at Hawke's Point, in the shadowy still water, if there was no shouting, and no splashing, and nobody there but me. I saw the little puffs of sand they made in the water, and ONCE I stepped on one, and it wriggled quickly away and slid under the sand, but I never saw one, so I kept quiet about them. I did not want to be told that I was mistaken, because I liked to believe it, but I kept it as a secret, and in doing so half admitted to myself that "Let's Pretend" was nearly over, and felt a slight regret for what had been such fun. Eleanor and I had even pretended that nasturtium flowers were ice cream cones, licking the air above them with great satisfaction!

She and I had a blissful time together, and I am happy that we can both remember it, because it came to an end when, in early 1917, father applied for and accepted a position as Excise Officer in Birmingham. He told me that we should be going on a long journey by train, over a wonderful bridge built by someone called ISAMBARD

KINGDOM BRUNEL, and that Birmingham was a fine town. So Toby went to live with Janey, and after saying "Goodbye" to everyone we set out for a new adventure.

Mary took this photograph of her parents when she was seven years old.

MARY BAKER

Born in 1910 in Derby, Mary Schofield Green, as she then was, was taken to Cornwall in November 1912 and went to live at Lelant in January 1913. In November 1916 the family moved to Birmingham, where Mary attended the King Edward's High School for Girls from 1921 to 1927.

In January 1928 the Greens returned to Lelant, and the following year Mary trained as a hand-loom weaver with Florence Welch at the Cottage Shop at the wharf, St Ives. She gave this up in 1933, soon after her marriage. In 1937 her husband took a job in Dartmouth, where their third child was born in December of that year. Times were hard and money was scarce, so early in 1939 Mary opened a small craft shop in Hauley Road, selling things that she made, such as children's clothes and toys. The war put an end to all that. Her husband joined the army and Mary went back to Lelant with the children.

Mary watches the second hand of a clock with her right hand
ready to switch on "The Archers" (1953 or 1954)
(Photo by courtesy of the "Birmingham Post & Mail")